W9-AYJ-763

A NIGERIAN FOLKTALE

WHY THE SKY IS FAR AWAY

Retold by Mary-Joan Gerson
Pictures by Carla Golembe

HARCOURT BRACE & COMPANY
Orlando Atlanta Austin Boston San Francisco Chicago Dallas New York
Toronto London

To Charles, Daniel, and Jessica
And to Nigeria
M.G.

To my husband, Joe Eudovich, whose love and encouragement
have helped me to realize my visions
Special thank you to Ann Rider and Susan Lu of Little, Brown
for their guidance and for being wonderful to work with
C.G.

Grateful acknowledgment is made to Ulli Beier for permission to adapt "Why the Sky Is Far Away,"
which appeared originally in *The Origin of Life and Death*, Heinemann, 1966.

This edition is published by special arrangement with Little, Brown and
Company (Inc.)

Grateful acknowledgment is made to Little, Brown and Company (Inc.) for
permission to reprint *Why The Sky Is Far Away*, retold by Mary-Joan
Gerson, illustrated by Carla Golembe. Text copyright © 1974, 1992 by Mary-Joan
Gerson; illustrations copyright © 1992 by Carla Golembe.

Printed in Mexico

ISBN 0-15-302135-7

2 3 4 5 6 7 8 9 10   050   97 96 95 94 93

In the beginning, the sky was very close to the earth.

In that time, men and women did not have to sow crops and harvest them. They did not have to prepare soup and cook rice. The children did not have to carry water from the stream or gather sticks for the fire. Anybody who was hungry just reached up, took a piece of sky, and ate it. It was delicious, too. Sometimes the sky tasted like meat stew, sometimes like roasted corn, and sometimes like ripe pineapple.

There was very little work to do, so people spent their time weaving beautiful cloth, carving handsome statues, and retelling tales of adventures. And there were always festivals to prepare for. The musicians practiced, the mask makers carved their masks in secret, and everywhere the children watched the preparations in wonder.

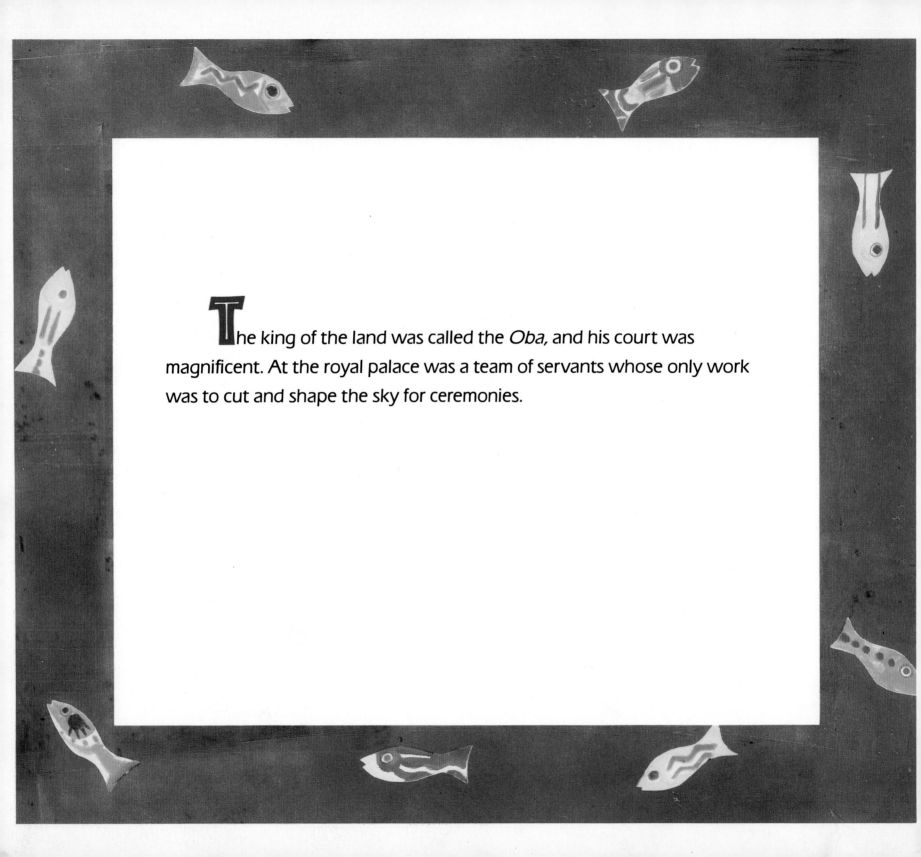

The king of the land was called the *Oba,* and his court was magnificent. At the royal palace was a team of servants whose only work was to cut and shape the sky for ceremonies.

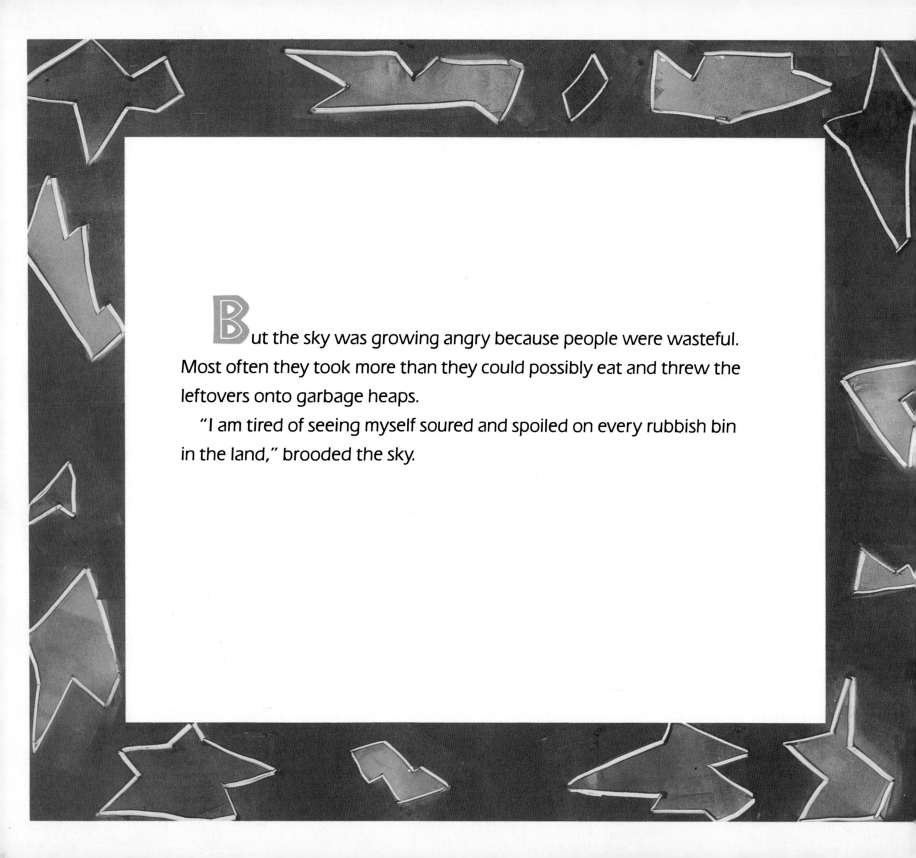

But the sky was growing angry because people were wasteful. Most often they took more than they could possibly eat and threw the leftovers onto garbage heaps.

"I am tired of seeing myself soured and spoiled on every rubbish bin in the land," brooded the sky.

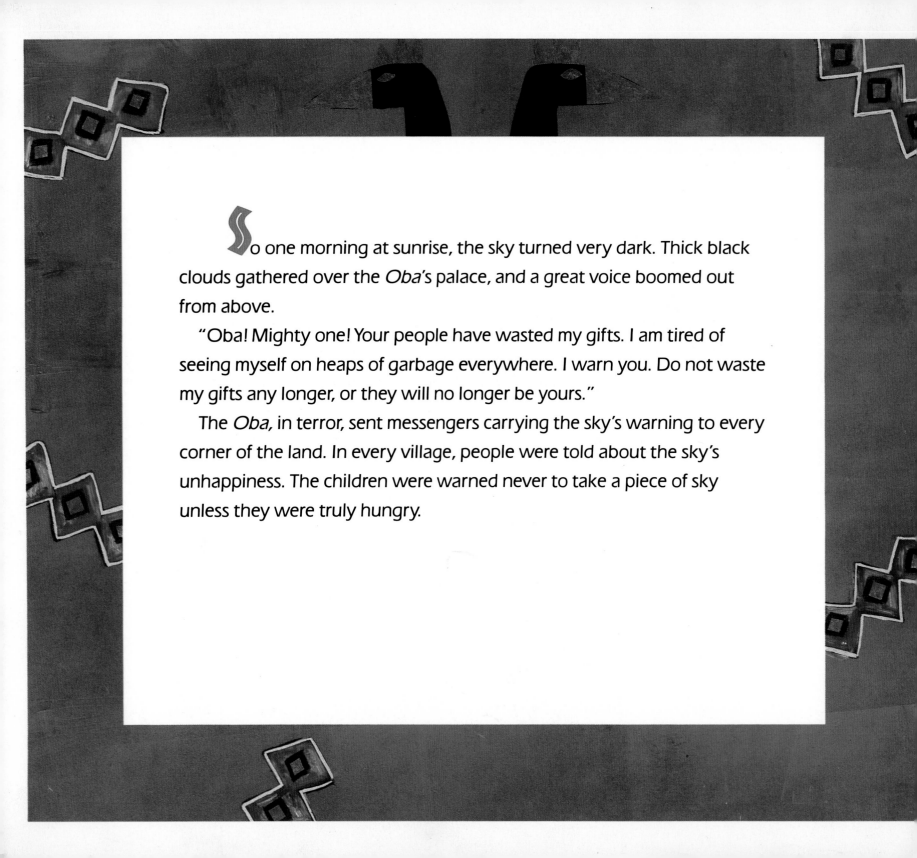

So one morning at sunrise, the sky turned very dark. Thick black clouds gathered over the *Oba*'s palace, and a great voice boomed out from above.

"Oba! Mighty one! Your people have wasted my gifts. I am tired of seeing myself on heaps of garbage everywhere. I warn you. Do not waste my gifts any longer, or they will no longer be yours."

The *Oba,* in terror, sent messengers carrying the sky's warning to every corner of the land. In every village, people were told about the sky's unhappiness. The children were warned never to take a piece of sky unless they were truly hungry.

People were very, very careful — that is, for a while. . . .

Then the time arrived for the greatest festival of the year. It was the festival that celebrated the power of the *Oba.*

The most important palace dancers performed all through the night, and the *Oba* himself, in ceremonial robes, danced for his subjects.

By the fifth day, there was rejoicing in every home and on every street. The *Oba* knew, though, that with the dancing and merriment, people might forget the sky's warning. So he made sure no one took more sky than he or she absolutely needed.

Now, there was a woman in this kingdom who was never satisfied. She could barely move when she wore all the weighty coral necklaces her husband had bought her, but she still craved more necklaces. She had eleven children of her own, but she felt her house was empty. And most of all, Adese loved to eat.

On the very last night of the celebration, Adese and her husband were invited to the *Oba's* palace. There they danced and danced and ate well past midnight.

What an evening it was," Adese thought later, standing in her own garden again. "How I wish I could relive tonight — the drumming I heard, the riches I saw, the food I ate!" She looked up at the sky and, hoping to taste again the cocoyams and meat stew the sky had offered, she took a huge piece to eat. She had only finished one-third of it when she could swallow no more.

"What have I done?" wailed Adese. "I cannot throw this away. Otolo!" she screamed, calling her husband. "Come and finish this piece of sky for me." Her husband, exhausted from dancing all night and stuffed with the sky he had eaten at the *Oba*'s palace, could take only two bites.

"Wake the children!" screamed Adese. Now, the children had spent all night at a masquerade and party after their dinner, and most of them were still too full to even nibble at their mother's piece of sky.

The neighbors were called, and the neighbors' neighbors were called, but Adese still held in her hand a big chunk of sky. "What does it matter," she said finally, "one more piece of sky on a rubbish heap." And just to make sure it didn't matter, she buried the leftover in the garbage bin at the back of her house.

Suddenly the ground shook with thunder. Lightning creased the sky above the *Oba's* palace, but no rain fell.

"Oba! Mighty one!" boomed a voice from above. "Your people have not treated me with respect. Now I will leave you and move far away."

"But what will we eat?" cried the *Oba*. "How will we live?"

"You must learn how to plow the land and gather crops and hunt in the forests," answered the sky. "Perhaps through your own labor you will learn not to waste the gifts of nature."

No one in the land slept very well that night. The rising sun uncovered the heads of men and women and children peering over rooftops and through windows, straining to see if the sky had really left them. It truly had. It had sailed upward, far out of their reach.

From that day onward, men and women and children had to grow their own food. They tilled the land and planted crops and harvested them. And far above them rested the sky, distant and blue, just as it does today.

AUTHOR'S NOTE

This story is at least five hundred years old. It was first told in Bini, the language of the Bini tribe of Nigeria, which has existed for more than eight hundred years. The Bini people live today, along with many other tribes, in what is now the country of Nigeria. How interesting it is that the Bini people long ago began teaching their children to respect the earth and sky. Today we are very concerned about caring for our planet. We now see, as the wise Bini did then, that the future of nature and its gifts rests in our own hands.